The Garden Birds Guide & Log Book

Edited by Ros Horton

Contents

Using this book	4
Grey heron	9
Mallard	10
Kestrel	12
Moorhen	14
Coot	15
Lapwing	16
Black-headed gull	18
Woodpigeon	19
Collared dove	20
Swift	21
Kingfisher	22
Green woodpecker	24
Great spotted woodpecker	25
Swallow	26
House martin	27
Pied wagtail	28
Starling	30
Magpie	32
Jay	34
Jackdaw	35
Rook	36
Crow	38
Wren	39

Robin 40

Blackbird 42

Song thrush 44

Mistle thrush 45

Blue tit 46

Great tit 48

Long-tailed tit 50

Coal tit 52

Nuthatch 53

House sparrow 54

Chaffinch 56

Greenfinch 58

Goldfinch 59

Log Book 60

Credits and acknowledgements 76

Using this book

When you look through this book you will soon see that on each page – or on a double page – we talk about a different bird. We tell you the main things that will help you recognise this bird. Sometimes there is something special about the way this particular bird behaves or looks that will help you to spot it quickly.

For each bird you will also find four different boxes giving other details:

In the **Appearance** box we tell you what the bird looks like – things like what colours the bird is on different parts of the body, how the bird stands or how you can spot it when flying.

The box called **Home** tells you about the kind of places you can find these birds living, so you know where to look for them.

In the **Food** box we tell you what this bird eats during different seasons of the year.

We will also tell you the kind of sounds to listen out for. Look for this symbol on the pages. Try saying the strange-looking words aloud just as they are written and you will get some idea of what this bird's call sounds like!

Birds in the garden

You can learn a lot about birds just by looking out of a window onto someone's garden. You are bound to spot common birds such as blackbirds, thrushes, robins and blue tits.

If your home has its own garden you can put food out in the winter such as peanuts or grated cheese as this will attract more and different types of birds. Make sure that you put food and bird baths in open places where cats cannot hide and then pounce on birds.

Where to look for birds

If you go to a park you can often see a wide range of birds, both on land and on water. Have a go at telling the difference between the different types of bird on the pond and watch how each different type behaves.

If you are looking for birds in the woods you need to learn to move quietly, using your ears as well as your eyes to spot birds. Use the bushes and trees to hide amongst so that birds are less likely to see you. Be patient and stay in one spot for a while. Once birds are used to you being there you have a better chance of watching them close up.

Ask your parents or teacher to arrange a visit to a nature reserve. These often have wardens working there who can give you help or even a guided walk. Joining an organisation like the Royal Society for the Protection of Birds (RSPB) can also help increase your knowledge.

Watching birds all through the year

It is fun to watch birds at any time of year but in some seasons there are more birds about in some places than others.

Spring is the breeding season and in the woods you will hear many different bird songs. If you want to listen to a huge variety of different birdsong you should get up very early – at dawn! If you go to the sea shore or river estuaries you will also catch sight of migrating birds coming in to join the birds who already live in this country.

In summer it can be quieter but if you go to lakes or reservoirs then you can see large flocks of swallows, martins and swifts feeding on insects there. Also, at the seaside there will be lots of hungry young seabirds being fed on the cliffs.

Autumn is an exciting time as at the coast many birds are migrating and in estuaries all kinds of ducks are gathering. As the weather gets worse towards winter, many birds move from inland to the coast because the sea makes the weather stay better and less extreme.

During the winter you will actually be able to see more birds and watch their behaviour more easily because there are fewer leaves on the trees and bushes. Also at this time many smaller birds roam about in flocks and are joined by birds visiting for the winter from abroad.

Equipment to help you watch birds

Although having good eyes and hearing are the best things for birdwatching, a pair of binoculars can be a great help. Try asking someone who knows about birds for advice about what sort is best for someone your age. Then add it to your Christmas or birthday list!

If you are going out for the day take a guidebook like this one with you and also a notepad. If you see an interesting bird but don't recognise it then jot down what size it is compared with other birds around it that you know already. Look for special marks or patterns. See what it looks like when flying or standing. Be aware of its beak shape. Listen to its call or make a note of any unusual behaviour. All these things will help you when you get back home and can look it up in a book or can ask someone what it was you saw.

By reading this book you will be able to answer questions like: 'Why are there so many sparrows everywhere?', 'Why is the female duck such a dull colour when the male is so bright and colourful?' and 'Why do I often see seagulls inland?'. As well as finding the answers to these questions you will also find lots of other unexpected details about birds.

We hope this book will help you to enjoy learning about birds and perhaps start you on an interest that will last all your life.

The birds

Grey heron

The silhouette of a heron standing still beside a river or pond is a memorable sight.

Herons are skilled hunting and fishing birds. They usually nest in tree-top colonies, although they do sometimes nest singly or on the ground.

There are around 5,000 breeding pairs in Britain, with the largest colony of 200 living at the RSPB Northward Hill reserve in Kent.

Home

You see them in ponds, lakes, rivers, marshes and other fresh-water sites, and sometimes at the coast, especially in winter.

Appearance

Herons are easy to recognise by their broad, rounded wings, kinked neck and long trailing legs. They have large, yellow dagger-shaped bills that turn pink when breeding.

Food

Herons eat fish, small mammals and birds, and can swallow even slippery eels.

Loud harsh **frank**

Both males and females have orange legs.

Mallard

Mallards are the most common form of duck and you will probably have seen some in your local park or on the village pond.

The female's brown feathers provide camouflage so that she stays hidden in vegetation while she nests. Mallards usually nest on the ground, laying between 9–13 bluish-green eggs. They often build nests away from water, sometimes high in a tree or on a building. In these cases the newly hatched young can have a difficult journey ahead of them to get to the water.

Appearance

The female has brown feathers, a yellowish bill and, like the male, orange legs. The male has a striking bottle-green head, white neck ring, purple-brown breast and grey back. In the summer his plumage changes to look more like the female's.

Home

You will find mallards almost anywhere there is water. They are to be seen in all kinds of places, from parks and ponds, reservoirs and gravel pits, to sea lochs and salt marshes.

Mallards are usually about 50–65cm long and can walk easily on dry land. Mallard drakes often defend territories around a small headland or similar.

In Britain there are probably more than 150,000 breeding pairs. In winter other mallards arrive from Europe, bringing the total to more than 700,000.

Food

Mallards feed on a varied diet and eat whatever they can find easily, such as water plants, seeds, grasses and insects. Town park ducks will eat almost anything offered to them.

 The female has a familiar **quack** and the male makes a weaker sound like **raehb**.

Downy chicks start to cheep as they hatch.

11

The handsome male kestrel. The female is much duller in colour than the male.

Kestrel

Kestrels are the most common bird of prey (or 'raptor') in Britain. You are quite likely to see them hovering over roadsides and motorway verges, but they can also be found in city centres.

Kestrels need open areas to hunt over, particularly grassy meadows and banks. They also need safe nesting sites, like holes in trees, cracks in walls or ledges on buildings. They sometimes also use an old crow's nest or nestboxes where provided.

 Kestrels make a **kee-kee-kee-kee** sound.

Appearance

The male has black flight-feathers contrasting with chestnut upperparts that can easily be spotted from a distance. Males also have a blue-grey head and a faint black 'moustache'. The tail has a visible black band.

12

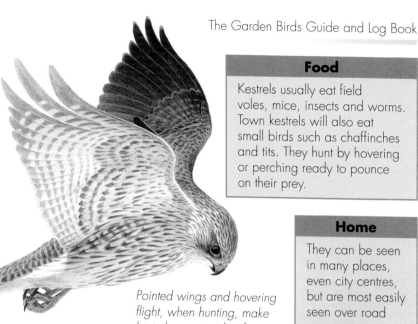

Food

Kestrels usually eat field voles, mice, insects and worms. Town kestrels will also eat small birds such as chaffinches and tits. They hunt by hovering or perching ready to pounce on their prey.

Home

They can be seen in many places, even city centres, but are most easily seen over road verges.

Pointed wings and hovering flight, when hunting, make kestrels easy to identify.

Kestrel population

The number of kestrels fell during the 1960s and 1970s because of the chemicals used in farming. However, the numbers have risen again and there are about 70,000 pairs nowadays.

What will still affect how many kestrels there are in the future is their supply of food. Changes in the way we farm in Britain mean there is less rough grazing land and this means that there are fewer small mammals available for kestrels to feed off.

Moorhen

Moorhens are water birds with long legs and big spread toes. They wade on marshy ground, swim well and walk or run on flat ground.

These birds jerk their head and tail as they swim along, looking out for danger.

Young moorhens have brown backs and a greenish bill.

Moorhens nest in trees or hedges, or in bushes beside water. They usually have two or three broods of black downy young each year.

♫ A quick **kittik** or a loud, sudden **kaak** and **kic-kic-kic**.

Food

They like water weeds, seeds, fruit, grasses, insects, worms and larvae.

Home

Moorhens live in fresh water with good plant cover, like small pools or large lakes or rivers.

Appearance

From a distance they look black and white but are really brownish black and grey. The bird's tail is held almost as high as the head.

Coot

Coots can be noisy birds and during the breeding season they have loud splashing fights with each other, and even with swans or geese.

Downy black and red chicks pester the adult birds for food.

♪ Coots have a loud and sudden call of *kep* or *coot*.

Coots swim well and can dive seven metres down.

In winter, you can see large flocks of these squabbling black and white birds diving together for food. Coots that spend the winter on ponds near humans often become very tame.

Coots have huge feet with long toes.

Home

Coots live on large open waters with plenty of vegetation and also on town-park ponds.

Food

They eat reed shoots, roots, algae, insects and eggs.

Appearance

Coots are black with white bills and white patches between the eyes. Their huge feet with long toes are visible when they run or fly across water.

15

♪ A rising, two-note, thin-sounding **wee-ip** or **pee-wit**.

Lapwing

The lapwing is a fairly large, rounded wader with a wispy crest. No other British bird has this particular plumage.

The lapwing is also known in England as the green plover and the peewit. 'Lapwing' describes its irregular, jerky flaps as it flies; 'green plover' refers to its plumage and 'peewit' is the sound it makes.

Home

In winter lapwings are mainly found on grassland and sometimes on ploughed fields but not on cold mountains or upland areas. During bad weather they will be by the coast and in summer are often found on wet meadows and moorland.

Appearance

Lapwings have broad rounded wings and a short blunt tail. In summer, males have an all-black chin, throat and breast and a longer black crest than females. Summer females have white speckling on the chin and throat and glossy blue-green wings, not dark-blue like males.

In winter there are over a million lapwings in Britain, some of which come from Europe. Lapwings are almost always found in flocks, often of several thousands of birds.

When the weather is bad, lapwings cover long distances in the day to find food. You might sometimes see them feeding by the side of the road, or even in your garden. When spring comes, lapwings can be seen in an amazing twisting and tumbling display flight.

Food

The lapwing eats a wide variety of fully grown insects and their larvae, many worms and some plants. Many of the things they eat would harm crops if not eaten.

Lapwings dig a scrape on dry land for their nest.

17

Black-headed gull

The sound of gulls is very familiar and you often see gleaming white flocks of them on fields, scrabbling over rubbish tips or in flight over the sea.

Many gulls breed inland but large colonies live on coastal marshes. In winter there may be three million of them, many from eastern Europe, with over a million living inland.

Adult black-headed gull in winter.

Appearance

Adults have a dark brown hood (from a distance this looks black), and red legs and bills, with white wings tipped with black. In winter, adults have a dark spot behind the eye.

Home

Gulls often live by the sea and marshes but are also found inland.

♫ Long squealing calls and short, yapping notes.

Food

Gulls are very adaptable and will eat worms, grubs, fish and scraps.

Woodpigeon

Although woodpigeons are large birds, they can be nervous and make sudden, noisy escapes with loud clattering wing-sounds.

Woodpigeons are tamer in the town than the country and nest at different times in each area because different types of food are available.

Home

Woodpigeons are found in farmland with trees, in woods and parks.

Appearance

These pigeons have a large chest and a long broad tail. They look grey at a distance but close up have a brown back, pink breast and attractive eye and bill colour. They have crescents of white on the wings and the neck.

♪ Woodpigeons make a series of sounds: *coo COOO coo, coo-coo* with the last having an extra *oo* at the end.

Food

These birds feed on the ground, eating leaves, seeds, berries, buds and grain.

Collared dove

A small, slim dove with long broad wings and a long tail, this bird arrived in Britain in the 1950s.

Their numbers have since increased massively in this country. Their breeding season is a long one and a single pair can rear between three and six broods of two young every year. They are social birds, who gather in flocks at good feeding sites and can be quite tame. If you have a birdtable in your garden, they are sure to visit.

Home

Collared doves are found in suburbs with conifers, parks, gardens, shrubberies, allotments and farms. They make their nests in trees, near the trunk.

Food

They eat grain, seeds and fruit.

Appearance

Pale grey-fawn with a pink breast and a thin black neck ring – the collar. In flight they use quick, rhythmic wing-beats and keep their wings quite arched.

♫ Continuous *ku-KOO-kuk* calls ending abruptly. In alarm or flight *kwurr* or *ghee-gheee*.

Swift

Appearance

Adults are dark sooty brown, almost black, with a pale chin. They have short, forked tails and small bills but, even though the bill is small, it can open up very wide to help the bird catch its insect food.

Swifts can be recognised by their familiar crescent-shaped wings, designed to help them make rapid but long flights.

Swifts are amazing birds that may fly well over a million miles during their ten-year life. When a young swift leaves the nest for the first, and only, time it flies to Africa immediately without its parents and may remain in flight non-stop for two or three years.

Long primary feathers and short inner wings are ideal for rapid flight.

Food

These birds eat insects and spiders in flight and eat up to 10,000 insects a day.

Home

Swifts can be seen anywhere in summer skies. They nest in older houses with rafters and often return to the same site every year.

 Swifts have a loud shrill scream.

Kingfisher

The kingfisher is Britain's most exotic-looking bird, but it is shy, and often the first sign you will have of it is its call, followed by a streak of electric blue flashing over the water.

Food

Kingfishers eat small fish but can manage those up to 8cm long, which they swallow head-first. Young birds need between 12 and 18 fish daily.

Kingfishers are hard to see when they perch quite still among vegetation, and when they dive for a fish they are lightning-quick. Where there are many small fish, kingfishers often make a catch four dives out of five and they can handle fish up to half their own body length.

A male kingfisher offers a fish to a female.

♪ Loud and shrill **chee** or angry **shrit-it-it**; especially vocal in spring and autumn.

22

Appearance

Kingfishers are small birds of 16–17cm, and their bill makes up about a quarter of their length. Male and female share the same colours of shiny blue, orange-red and white, with bright-red feet. The male bird's bill is all black, but the female has a red base to the lower part of the bill. Young birds are duller in colour with dark feet.

They nest in narrow tunnels about 60–90cm long dug out in banks over water, laying their eggs in a space at the end of the tunnel. These tunnels become very dirty with fish bones and pellets and you can often spot the entrance by the white droppings that collect below it. To clean this dirt off their plumage, adults usually plunge-bathe as soon as they leave the nest.

Kingfishers guard their territories fiercely and even chase their own young away just days after they have left the nest. They then start a second brood almost straight away.

Kingfishers wait patiently on a branch until they spot a fish, then they plunge into the water to catch their prey.

Home

You will find kingfishers in unpolluted, still or slow-flowing water in most of Britain, although they are quite rare in Scotland. Some move to estuaries or sheltered coasts in winter.

Green woodpecker

You will more often hear a green woodpecker than see one, as they are very shy birds. They can be hard to spot but their laughing call carries far.

This woodpecker is the largest of Britain's woodpeckers and can be identified in flight by its pointed head and tail and its bursts of flapping followed by long swooping glides.

Home

These birds are found in deciduous woods, parkland, heaths and commons. Sometimes also seen in well-wooded gardens.

Appearance

This bird has green plumage, a striking red crown and a yellow rump, best seen in flight. They have dark cheeks and a pale eye-ring.

Food

Woodpeckers mainly eat ants and their pupae, using their beak and long sticky-tipped tongue to dig them out of the ants' nest.

♫ Loud *yaffle* sound or rapid screeching notes when disturbed.

24

Home

Widely found in woodland, hedgerow trees and gardens, this bird builds its nest in decaying wood.

Food

They eat insects, larvae and seeds, usually high in woodland trees. In spring, the young are fed on caterpillars.

Appearance

This bird is about the size of a blackbird and has a black, white and red plumage. A male bird has a brilliant red patch on the back of his neck.

Great spotted woodpecker

This woodpecker spends most of its time high in the trees searching out insects by using rapid beak movements.

In spring they prefers dense woodland, but at other times the birds can be found high in any high tree or copse. Its territorial drumming is often accompanied by aerial chases through the trees with two or three birds chattering loudly.

♪ Loud repeated *tchik*; and rattling trill.

Swallow

The swallow is well known for its beautiful, deeply forked tail. These long tails help the birds to fly easily over ground and water.

Britain's swallows go to Africa in winter and return between March and May. They build their nests of mud and dry grass, often on ledges in outbuildings. Sometimes they use the same nests several years running, which tells us a lot about their amazing ability to navigate their way around the world.

A nest built under the eaves of an outbuilding.

Food

Swallows catch flies and butterflies which they eat while they are flying.

Home

Swallows are found in open country, but can also live near buildings.

Appearance

Males have longer tail feathers than females. Swallows are glossy blue-black on top with pale undersides, and a blue band across the breast. Their throats and foreheads are a rich, deep red.

♪ *Tswit-tswit*; alarm call *tswee*.

Swallows can often be seen gathered on wires in the early autumn, before they migrate south.

26

House martin

You will often see house martins flying to and from their nests under house eaves in villages, towns and city suburbs.

They build cup-shaped nests mainly of mud, which they gather in their bills and apply with trembling chin movements. They are very social birds and often dozens of nests are built together.

Food

House martins eat insects while in flight. Parents feed the young both in the air and perched on wires.

Adults eat insects while in flight.

Gathering mud for nest building.

Appearance

Adults are blue-black with bright-white underparts and white feathers on their short legs. Sometimes the upperpart looks jet black. The young are browner above and below.

♪ A **chrrrp** sound. Their sound of alarm is a shrill **treep**.

Home

These birds live around houses and over open areas and wetlands, sometimes nesting on cliffs. House martins spend the winter in Africa and arrive in this country each spring.

Pied wagtail

You can spot pied wagtails by their black and white plumage and their constantly bobbing tails as they chase across short grass in search of insects.

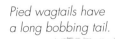

Pied wagtails have a long bobbing tail.

 A twittering warble and a shrill-sounding **tchissick, tchuwee**.

Appearance

The pied wagtail has a greyer back and a white throat in winter but keeps the crescent of black on the breast. Females have a greyer back and a smaller bib than males. You will notice the wagtail's long tail and distinctive call, especially when it is flying.

These birds are often seen trotting along the ground in paddocks and fields, dashing after insects scared up by horses or cattle. They are also found in school playing-fields and flying at dusk towards their communal roost, where hundreds gather noisily on a tree before flying to a reed bed, bush or even a building ledge for the night.

They prefer short grass, and tarmac, where they can run along the ground but they are agile birds and can dart rapidly or fly up to catch passing insects.

Food

These birds eat insects and seeds.

Habits

In winter, northern birds move down to southern England, some going to France, Spain or Morocco. Pied wagtails breed all over Britain apart from the Shetland Isles. They build nests in holes in walls, sheds, banks and ivy using grass and moss and lining these with feathers and hair. They lay 5–6 pale-grey, speckled eggs.

These birds protect their territory very fiercely in spring and will even attack their own reflections in the mirrors and hubcaps of parked cars!

The birds dart rapidly at passing insects.

Home

Pied wagtails can be found in open country, especially farmyards, parks and gardens, and often near water.

A female pied wagtail.

Starling

Flocks of black starlings are a very familiar sight in gardens, parks and town centres.

What is less familiar are some of the facts about their mating habits. In spring, male birds build rough nests in holes in buildings or trees and then sing with a puffed-out throat and drooped wings to attract a mate. If a female comes close he will sing while waving his wings frantically and with his tail fanned.

If she stops nearby he will sing from the nest itself to attract her in. Once she is inside, she will finish the lining of the nest.

Females lay 4–6 eggs and sometimes lay an egg in another starling's nest.

♪ Starlings are known for their long mixture of trills, rattles and screeching calls.

Food

These birds eat seeds, fruit, caterpillars, ants and leather-jackets (you might know them better as daddy-long-legs).

Many starlings mimic the songs of other birds.

Home

Starlings are found everywhere, including gardens, parks and town centres.

Starlings are a common sight in gardens.

Appearance

In spring the male is very glossy and colourful with a blue base to the beak (the female has a pink patch on her bill). From December the bill turns yellow and in spring the starling's legs change from dull brown to orange or red. Starlings wave their wings energetically when singing.

Sometimes you might come across one of these bright-blue eggs on a lawn, removed from a nest by a starling.

Some males have several mates and leave one mate on her eggs and go off with another younger female. The male sits on the eggs for a short period of the day and the female sits on them for rest of the day and all night.

The starling's distinctive plumage emerges as it reaches adulthood.

Appearance

The magpie's black feathers are actually purplish-blue and the tail is shiny green with a band of reddish-purple at the tip. Their bill, legs and feet are black and they have dark brown eyes. On the ground they hold their tails up high and rarely spread them.

Food

In winter magpies eat seeds and berries, and all year round they feed on animals killed by road traffic. They hoard food by burying it, returning to eat it a few days later.

Magpie

There's no mistaking a magpie – its black and white feathers and long tail immediately gives it away. They also make a memorable sound like the noise of a machine gun.

Magpies look rather comic when they are on the ground because they lift their legs in high steps and hop or bounce sideways if they are excited or looking for food.

Magpies can lay up to eight eggs. Young magpies find it hard to fly and stay hidden in vegetation. The family group stays together until the autumn.

32

Home

Magpies are found in many places such as farmland and open country but prefer grassland with thick hedges or scattered trees. Numbers have recently increased in towns and suburbs. There are fewer in eastern England where many hedges have been removed.

Bad reputation

These birds are unpopular with some people, who say that magpies eat too many eggs and young of other small birds (though they do less damage than cats and eat fewer birds than hawks and falcons do).

Magpies are common in Britain apart from parts of Scotland. They do not move away from their home territories and no other magpies from Europe join them in winter.

The magpie's black and white feathers and long tail are unmistakeable.

Young magpies have very short tails.

 A loud, fast **chak-chak-chak**.

33

Jay

Jays are easily disturbed and are most often seen flying away!

Although jays sometimes take nuts and fat from bird feeders in rural gardens, they are wary of humans. Jays bury thousands of acorns, which ensures a good food supply and the future survival of oak woods.

 A harsh **skraak** or a quiet mewing sound.

Appearance

Jays are the most colourful member of the crow family, with a pinkish-brown body, blue and black wings, white rump and black tail. The crown is whitish, streaked black and forms a small crest when standing upright.

Home

Jays are found in large numbers in wooded parts of England and Wales such as deciduous and coniferous woods, farmland, parks, gardens and suburbs.

Food

Jays eat all kinds of foods but they are especially fond of acorns.

Appearance

Jackdaws are black except for some grey on the neck and head, and a pale-coloured eye. When defending their nest sites they fluff out their feathers and spread their tails.

Jackdaw

Jackdaws are sociable birds and often roost and feed with other crows, especially rooks.

Noisy and sometimes aggressive, jackdaws are quicker and more active on the ground and in the air than other crows. They nest in colonies in large holes in trees or cliffs.

Home

You will find jackdaws in towns, cities, on farmland, parkland, woodland and sea cliffs.

Food

These birds eat almost anything, including grain and seeds and sudden, plentiful food supplies such as leaf-eating caterpillars in May or June. They often scavenge at domestic refuse tips in winter.

A *jak* sound, as well as *kow* and *chuk-chuk*.

Rook

The sound of rooks cawing from tree-tops is a well-loved part of country life. This familiar noise often comes from collections of many nests built together in tree-tops and known as a 'rookery'.

Rooks are sociable birds that gather together in groups of several thousand birds in rookeries. You are also quite likely to see them flying together as roaming flocks of big black birds. They are at their most active and noisy in the rookery in the springtime when they quarrel over their territories and chase each other round the rookery. They also display themselves by bowing, fanning their tails and drooping their wings.

Appearance

Rooks appear to be completely black but in fact their feathers have a purplish tint. They have long feathers on their thighs, which makes them look as though they are wearing baggy trousers! The face and chin of adults is without feathers and is pale grey. The base of the bill is also grey. When these birds are viewed against the sun their feathers appear silvery.

Food

Rooks are often blamed for damaging crops, and they certainly do eat grain, but they actually mainly eat worms and leatherjackets (better known as daddy-long-legs).

Rooks reuse nests made from sticks the previous year. They usually lay between four and five eggs but can lay as many as seven.

Rooks are known for their deep **caw** or **kaaah**.

Single rooks can be seen walking carefully on the ground looking for seeds and insects but they also feed together in large groups. They are often joined in their roosts and rookeries by jackdaws and carrion crows. In the winter rooks come over from Europe to join those that are already here.

Home

Rooks live in farmland, parks, grasslands and wooded suburbs.

Rooks are very sociable, and live in large communal roosts.

Crow

The all-black carrion crow is found throughout England and Wales but in Scotland, Ireland and the Isle of Man there are hooded crows instead. Both belong to the European crow family and sometimes breed with each other.

Crows are often confused with rooks. The way to tell them apart is by the fact that rooks are normally seen in large groups while crows are usually on their own or in pairs.

Appearance

The carrion crow is completely black (including its beak) with a blue and green gloss. The hooded crow has a grey body and black head. They have strong dagger-shaped bills, good for eating the flesh of dead animals ('carrion').

The all-black carrion crow.

Home

Found in many places including farmland, the coast, towns, parks and open woodland.

Food

Crows eat all kinds of things including gamebird eggs and rubbish from tips and the shoreline.

Well known for their **kaaaw**.

38

Wren

People often don't realise that the wren is the most common British bird, with about ten million pairs living here.

Although there are many wrens, if there is a bad winter they often die from lack of food. You can help by sprinkling grated cheese under hedges and other low places.

Wrens have a very loud song for such a small bird.

♪ A hard *chiti* or dry rattle.

Wrens' nests are ball-shaped structures with a neat opening on one side.

Appearance

Wrens are red-brown above with darker bars and beige below. They have a short, upright (cocked) tail. Males, females and young birds all look alike.

Home

You find wrens in gardens, remote sea cliffs and woodlands. Although often invisible in the undergrowth, they do pop out to sing.

Food

Wrens eat live insect larvae and spiders. In winter they may eat cheese or suet.

Robin

Robins are often seen perched on the handle of a spade in the garden and you will know them at once by the red patch on the breast. You will also certainly have seen them pictured on Christmas cards!

Robins can live up to ten years but only a quarter usually live beyond their first birthday. Their greatest enemies are cats and road traffic, which kill a lot of them every year.

Male and female robins look the same. You will hear them singing to mark out their territories.

Robins look for mating partners between December and March, with the female chasing the male until he accepts her. Once they become a pair, the male feeds the female. The female lays 5–7 red-spotted white eggs.

Home

You will find robins in gardens, woods and hedges. They nest in hedges, banks, ledges or nest-boxes. Sometimes they choose surprising nesting places such as old kettles or garden sheds!

Food

Although they mainly eat insects, robins also like fruit and seeds. They are very fond of mealworms and can become hand tame if fed with them.

Appearance

They are known for their red breast, and both male and female robins look the same. The young are spotted with no red breast, but grow adult feathers in the autumn. Robins stand very upright, and they bob their heads and flick their wings and tail when excited.

Territorial birds

When nesting, the male robin defends his territory strongly. Fights between males can be fierce, and may even lead to death.

In very cold winters robins are less concerned to fight for their territories and often several birds will then feed together on a birdtable.

Robins have a lovely sad song, which is strong in spring and quieter in autumn.

 A beautiful song and a *tic-tic-tic* call.

Young robins have spotted feathers, but get their adult feathers and red breast in the autumn.

Blackbird

You will see blackbirds in Britain throughout the year. They are often found searching a lawn with head cocked and then slowly but surely pulling out a struggling worm.

As they search for food, blackbirds move about in short, hopping runs. When they cock their heads they look as if they are listening for food but in fact they are looking for it.

 Clear fluting notes in phrases lasting about six seconds, with pauses of the same length in between.

Appearance

The male is strongly black though the wings look paler when flapped. Females are sooty brown with pale streaked throats. The legs of both are dark. Many blackbirds have quite a few white feathers and some are albino (pure white).

Home

Blackbirds live in dense woodland and moorland, and are common in gardens.

Blackbirds are often seen searching the lawn for worms.

Blackbirds eat a lot of fruit and berries in the winter. If the ground stays soft, worms are their main diet.

They sing between March and June, from a song post. When they spot danger, they have a rattling alarm sound.

Blackbirds nest a little way up in trees and hedges, sometimes in buildings. They build nests of mud and moss lined with grass, in which the females lay 3–5, bluish-green, speckled brown eggs.

Migration
Every autumn migrant blackbirds come from northern Europe. In late October and November many arrive on the east coast of Britain and you can see hundreds of blackbirds, along with thrushes,

Food
Blackbirds feed mainly on the ground. In the summer they eat insects and in the winter berries and fruit but if the ground is soft then they mainly eat worms.

dropping from the sky. These migrants join the other birds that live here all year round and they all feed together. Orchards with rotting apples are a favourite feeding ground for these birds.

Appearance

Song thrushes have brown upperparts and a pale-brown breast covered in small narrow black spots. They stand quite upright, with long legs. When running they crouch more horizontally.

Food

They eat worms, snails, fruit and berries. Putting grated cheese or fruit on a birdtable attracts them.

Song thrush

Smashed snail shells on a garden path are a sign that song thrushes have been around! They are the only bird that gets to its food like this.

Although there used to be more song thrushes than blackbirds this is now the other way round. Thrushes are often seen collecting food below birdtables.

Home

Song thrushes live in gardens, hedgerows and woodland.

 Thrushes sing their lovely song from low bushes or buildings. When alarmed they give a rattle, and in flight a thin *sip*.

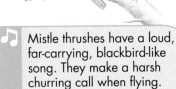

Mistle thrush

You can tell mistle thrushes by the big, round spots on their underparts and the pure white underwing that is clearly seen when they are flying.

Mistle thrushes move about with strong hopping leaps. They stand very upright and can be quite angry birds, unafraid to drive cats and dogs away from nests. They sometimes even hit human beings on the head in their own gardens if there are nests about!

♪ Mistle thrushes have a loud, far-carrying, blackbird-like song. They make a harsh churring call when flying.

Home

You find them in gardens and woodland.

Food

They eat fruit, berries and insects.

Appearance

These are larger than song thrushes and have a greyer back and bigger spots.

Blue tit

These little birds are known for stealing cream from milk bottles, for pecking at putty, and even for tearing wallpaper if given the chance!

Bluetits are very active and acrobatic little birds. This means they can find food at the end of the thinnest twigs, unlike the bigger great tit.

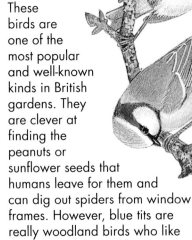

Blue tits are great acrobats.

Home

You will find blue tits in woods, especially where there are oak and birch trees. In winter they are widespread in gardens.

Blue tits will steal the cream from the top of milk bottles if they get the chance.

These birds are one of the most popular and well-known kinds in British gardens. They are clever at finding the peanuts or sunflower seeds that humans leave for them and can dig out spiders from window frames. However, blue tits are really woodland birds who like to live in oak or birch trees.

Food

Blue tits eat insects in summer, and insects and seeds in the winter.

Young blue tits have greeny caps and yellow faces.

Nesting

Blue tits produce only one brood of chicks each year, just at the time when there are lots of juicy caterpillars about. This means that if the brood fails to grow up for any reason there is no second chance that year. This is different from the blackbird, who has three or four broods spread throughout the summer.

High, thin notes, churrs and trills – *tsee, tsee-see-chuchuchuch*.

Blue tits nest in trees, nestboxes, and almost any kind of hole, and lay between 7 and 13 tiny white eggs with red-brown spots.

Appearance

The blue tit has a bright blue cap, blue wings and tail, a clean yellow breast and an underside with a thin dark streak. They have white faces with black lines on them. Young birds have yellow faces and greener caps than their parents.

Great tit

**If you watch a group of
birds on a bird-table you
will be able to tell great tits
easily because they can be
quite rough.**

You can spot these tits by their large
size, and their white cheeks, yellow
breast, and black crown and bib.
They have strong beaks used to break
open hazelnuts and also as a weapon.
Great tits have even been known to
kill and eat parts of other birds.

Home

You will find great tits in
woods, hedges and gardens.

Food

Great tits
mainly eat
insects (especially
caterpillars), seeds
and fruit. You often
see them
on the ground
in woods tossing
leaves aside and
tearing up moss
in search of food.

*A great tit searching
for food under
some leaves.*

48

Appearance

You can tell the male from the female by the thick black band on his belly, which carries on between his legs. Females have less black on the belly. The great tit's tail is blue-grey with white outer feathers.

Unusual nest sites

These birds nest in unusual sites such as pipes and letterboxes. The males don't help build the nest but they do feed the female (the 'hen') when she is laying and looking after the eggs. If the female is disturbed in her nest she will hiss like a snake to frighten away enemies.

Like other tits, great tits feed their young on caterpillers and plan to have their families when there are lots of these about. Like blue tits, great tits have learned to open milk bottles and when tested in special experiments they can carry out very difficult tasks to get hold of food.

Young great tits have duller colours than adult birds, and their cheeks are pale yellow, not white.

They have a very wide range of different calls. Many of these have a ringing sound, such as **chink**. Their song is a loud **teacheteacher-teacher**.

Appearance

These birds have fluffy plumage. Adults are black, white and pale pink. The young have no pink, dark cheeks and shorter tails.

Long-tailed tits can be recognised by their 'ball and stick' shape when perching and flying.

🎵 These birds make a thin *zi-zi-zi*; **tup** and a **trrr**. They rarely sing.

Long-tailed tit

You can tell these birds by their unusual shape, which is like a ball and stick – a small round body and a long tail.

These birds are good acrobats and can hang upside down by one foot while holding bits of food in the other foot and eating them.

These are social birds and, after the breeding season, you can see flocks of them wandering through woods and along hedges, with other tits and small birds. They move quickly through trees and bushes, crossing any gaps in single file and calling non-stop as they go.
In winter a flock will defend its territory against other flocks and roost together, huddling together for warmth.

Home

Long-tailed tits live in hedges, bushes and woods in the winter.

Long-tailed tits are very social birds and you can often see them moving quickly through trees and bushes.

Nesting

The nest they build is different from other birds' and is a bit like a stretchy, oval purse of moss, webs and lichen and lined with hundreds of feathers. They sometimes take up to 20 days to build this, often in a fork of a tree or hedge. These birds like tight places and both parents will fit into the nest with up to a dozen young. They lay between 8 and 12 white, red-spotted eggs.

Long-tailed tits rarely come to birdtables but if they do they may then come regularly, sometimes for several winters.

Food

These tits eat mainly insects but they also peck lichen from trunks and branches.

Coal tit

This bird is most often seen in woods where there are conifers, and they often flit around the top of pine trees.

The coal tit is the smallest of the tits and can look a bit dumpy and short-tailed. In the winter this bird often visits gardens, taking small pieces of food dropped by other birds.

Young coal tits have yellower cheeks than the adults.

Food

They eat mainly insects and seeds.

Home

Coal tits live in woods, especially coniferous ones, and gardens. They nest in hollows among the roots of trees or even in mouse-holes.

Appearance

They have a double bar on their wings and a larger black bib than other small tits. You can also tell them by the large, white patch on the back of their neck.

A bright **peet** sound. Their song is like a great tit's but faster and softer.

These birds make a number of different whistle sounds that sound like *chwit-chwit*, *tsirrup* and *twee*.

Appearance

The most striking thing about these birds is the broad, black eye-stripe. Their bodies are blue-grey above and pale brown below.

Nuthatch

This is a big-headed, short-tailed, perky little bird, a bit like a tiny woodpecker in shape and behaviour and always on the move.

Nuthatches are unusual because they can climb down tree trunks and branches as well as up them. They also plaster their nest-hole entrances with hard-drying mud to keep out enemies like weasels. Nuthatches open nuts by pushing them into bark and then breaking them open with noisy bangs from their bill.

Food

These birds eat insects, nuts and seeds, especially beechnuts, acorns and hazelnuts.

Home

Nuthatches are found in woods and parks.

House sparrow

This very well-known little bird is good at finding and living alongside humans. It has cleverly learned to make the most of human rubbish and food that has been thrown away.

You will see sparrows anywhere, from the centre of large cities to farm buildings far out in the county. Sparrows have spread throughout the world, often by following European explorers. These birds travelled to the African desert in World War 2 by following army camps.

Food

These birds eat a variety of food, mainly seeds and buds. Food provided in gardens will attract many house sparrows, which have learned to feed from peanut feeders.

Home

Sparrows are often found near human settlements in both town and country. They build untidy grass and straw nests in buildings or hedges.

Putting food out in the garden will always attract large numbers of house sparrows.

Male sparrows show off the contrast in their feathers when flying. Females are much plainer.

 Sparrows make noisy twittering and cheeping notes that sound like ***chissick***.

They have also been seen taking rides on the London Underground and on cross-Channel ferries where waste scraps of food are easy to find. Sparrows appear in all kinds of remote places where people settle but we don't always know how the sparrows find these!

Sparrows usually breed from May to July with three broods. Now, they are starting to breed the whole year round whenever there is a spell of fine weather. This means you can even see young fledglings in the middle of winter. They lay 3–7 finely speckled and greyish eggs.

Appearance

On the ground, sparrows move in hops or shuffles. They have brown backs and wings with white bars and a grey rump. The male has eye-catching feathers that are duller in winter than spring. The female and young are duller in colour.

55

Chaffinch

Chaffinches are known and loved for their springtime singing and are one of Britain's most common birds.

There are over seven million pairs of chaffinches in Britain and Ireland. The ones who live in Britain rarely move about three miles from home but they are joined in winter by birds from Europe who may have travelled 1,200 miles to get here.

 They make a *spink* call, a *choop* in flight and have a rattling song that ends with a flourish.

Appearance

These colourful birds can be identified in flight by their white outer tail feathers and the white bars on their wings. The male has a pink breast and grey head. The female is pale brown and grey.

We think that about 10 to 20 million chaffinches come from Europe each autumn. You can watch huge numbers of birds arriving on the east and south coasts during October and November. These winter flocks can be heard by their choop sound.

The white bars on the wings and the white tail feathers of the chaffinch can easily be seen when flying.

Food

Chaffinches eat a variety of food.

The male chaffinch has a pink breast and a grey head. Females are pale brown and grey.

Chaffinches feed on the ground and can be seen in flocks in open countryside searching for seeds to eat. They only produce one brood a year. For this they build a well-camouflaged nest out of grass and lichen in the fork of a tree or dense bush. In this they lay four or five greenish, dark-spotted eggs.

They live a long time for such a small bird, possibly up to 12 years. Unfortunately, many birds are killed by traffic or by cats.

Home

You will find chaffinches in hedgerows, gardens and farmland. They nest in bushes or low trees.

Greenfinch

These greeny yellow birds are a familiar sight nowadays on birdtables. They visit these because they like sunflower seeds, the peanut feeders and other goodies.

Greenfinches, like sparrows, are confident birds and can be rough when competing for food. They will often drive away other, shyer birds by their roughness. They have a wide bill and short well-forked tail. The bill helps them to eat large seeds.

Appearance

The male has olive-green plumage and older ones have more yellowy feathers. The female is brown with yellow patches on the wings.

Greenfinches have a twittering song and make a nasal *tsweee* sound.

Home

You will find greenfinches in open woodland, gardens and farmland.

Food

These birds eat mainly seeds and berries, particularly yew and cotoneaster berries.

Goldfinch

 Twittering calls and song – *tswitt-witt-witt*.

These birds get their name from the bright yellow flash that stands out clearly on their black wings when they are flying.

This thin delicate finch sometimes flutters rather like a butterfly in low vegetation. They like plants on open ground and although they can hop on the ground they are more often seen hanging from seedheads.

Food

Goldfinches eat insects and seeds, particularly thistle seeds.

Home

Goldfinches are found in gardens, orchards and rough and open ground. They build nests of wool and moss at branch ends.

Appearance

These birds can be recognised easily by the contrast of the yellow bar on their black wing feathers. Goldfinches also have a pattern on their head that is very noticeable. The male birds have a bright red patch that ends just behind the eye.

The Garden Birds Guide and Log Book

Species	M	F	J	No	Location

Time	Date	Weather condition and other notes

The Garden Birds Guide and Log Book

Species	M	F	J	No	Location

Time	Date	Weather condition and other notes

The Garden Birds Guide and Log Book

Species	M	F	J	No	Location

Time	Date	Weather condition and other notes

The Garden Birds Guide and Log Book

Species	M	F	J	No	Location

Time	Date	Weather condition and other notes

The Garden Birds Guide and Log Book

Species	M	F	J	No	Location

Time	Date	Weather condition and other notes

The Garden Birds Guide and Log Book

Species	M	F	J	No	Location

Time	Date	Weather condition and other notes

The Garden Birds Guide and Log Book

Species	M	F	J	No	Location

Time	Date	Weather condition and other notes

The Garden Birds Guide and Log Book

Species	M	F	J	No	Location

Time	Date	Weather condition and other notes

Published by AA Publishing (a trading name of Automobile Association Developments Limited, whose registered office is Fanum House, Basing View, Basingstoke, Hampshire RG21 4EA; registered number 1878835)

ISBN 978-0-7495-6022-5

A03924

A CIP catalogue record for this book is available from the British Library.

The contents of this book are believed correct at the time of printing. Nevertheless, the publishers cannot be held responsible for any errors, omissions or for changes in the details given in this book or for the consequences of any reliance on the information provided by the same. This does not affect your statutory rights. We have tried to ensure accuracy in this book but things do change and we would be grateful if readers would advise us of any inaccuracies they may encounter.

www.theAA.com/travel

Layouts and editorial for AA Publishing by Pentacor Book Design, High Wycombe, Bucks

Printed and bound in China

Acknowledgements:

All images are held in the Association's library (AA World Travel Library) with contributions from:

N Arlott 6, 7, 24, 28/9, 30tr, 39, 50

T Boyer 2, 8, 10/11, 30c, 31tl, 31br, 32/3, 33b, 34, 35, 36/7, 38, 42/3, 44, 45

H Burn 11tr, 16, 17

J Gale 14tr

R Gillmor 9

P Hayman 3, 46/7, 48/9, 52, 54/5, 56/7, 58, 59

I Lewington 41br

D Quinn 13b, 18b

D Rees 33t

C Rose 1,4, 12, 13t, 14c, 15, 18tl, 18cr, 19, 20, 21, 22/3, 26, 40/1, 53

Cover Acknowledgements:

Abbreviations for the picture credits are as follows: (t) top; (b) bottom; (l) left; (r) right; (AA) AA World Travel Library.

Front Cover AA/P Hayman; Back Cover (l) AA/C Rose; Back Cover (tr) AA/N Arlott; Back Cover (br) AA/N Arlott;

Every effort has been made to trace the copyright holders, and we apologise in advance for any accidental errors. We would be happy to apply the corrections in the following edition of this publication.